Bradwell's B

Scotland

a Feast of **Fun**, **Facts** and **History!**

Published by Bradwell Books
11 Orgreave Close Sheffield S13 9NP
Email: books@bradwellbooks.co.uk

Compiled by Camilla Zajac

British Library Cataloguing in Publication Data:
a catalogue record for this book is available from the
British Library.

1st Edition

ISBN: 9781912060566

Design by: Andrew Caffrey

Print: Gomer Press, Llandysul, Ceredigion SA44 4JL

Photograph Credits: iStock, Creative Commons (CC)
and credited individually.

Cover Photographs Credits: Left - Right. iStock, iStock,
iStock, Thomas Rodger, iStock & iStock. Main iStock.

BIOGRAPHY

CAMILLA ZAJAC is an author and
copywriter who wrangles with words
for publishers and companies in sectors
as varied as engineering, telematics
and manufacturing. She is not afraid to
admit that not only did she try a deep-
fried Mars bar when visiting Glasgow,
but she also enjoyed it.

Find out more at:
www.greenlightcopywriting.co.uk

Bradwell's Book of

Scotland

a Feast of **Fun, Facts** and **History!**

BRADWELL
BOOKS

Contents

FAMOUS LOCALS

Whether it's helping to create the National Health Service, changing the face of football or creating one of the world's most important inventions, Scottish people have helped to influence events around the world.

SCOTTISH SPORT

As you would expect for the birthplace of golf and league football, sport has a special place in Scotland's heart. Find out about these and other more unusual outdoor activities enjoyed in Scotland.

LOCAL NAMES AND CLANS

Many Scottish families can claim a connection with one of the country's clans, and the long and proud history that they represent. Each clan has its own tartan, the wearing of which became popular in Victorian times.

MURDER STORIES

Many of us have heard of Burke and Hare, but did you know the full story of their infamous exploits? Read on to find out more and to hear about another tragic true murder tale from Scotland's past.

LOCAL CUSTOMS

There are many colourful and long-established customs to be found around Scotland, some of which, such as Hogmanay and Burns Night, are celebrated around the world.

SCOTTISH HISTORY

Scotland's fascinating history combines biscuits, banking and beer. From ancient monastic traditions to the industrial boom, the history of Scotland is an undeniably rich one.

Introduction

SAY THE NAME 'SCOTLAND' AND MANY ASSOCIATIONS SPRING TO MIND. FROM WHISKY TO TARTAN AND FROM HAGGIS TO HOGMANAY.

While all those aspects are very important to Scotland, it is when you look beyond them that you can discover an even richer national identity. Scotland's ancient roots help to make it a country of drama, energy and character.

What else would you expect from the country that is the birthplace of golf? Known historically as Caledonia and by the Gaelic name Alba, Scotland has seen many achievements and firsts in its time, whether that's the world's first colour photograph, the first successfully cloned lifeform (remember *Dolly the sheep?*) or the establishment of the world's oldest transport company.

You might think you know Scotland, but were you aware that the unicorn is its national animal? This is less surprising than it might at first seem when you consider that Scotland has a long heritage of myth and legend. The unicorn has been a Scottish heraldic symbol since the 12th century, when William I had it included on an early form of the Scottish coat of arms. Maintaining a connection with the past is still very much central to Scotland's identity. As you'll see in this book, some of Scotland's oldest traditions are still alive and well today.

Scottish culture, people and products have helped to shape events around the world. Whether it is the creation of the world's first synthetic plastic or the identity of the most popular of DOCTOR WHO'S companions, the Scottish people continue to achieve great things. And let's not forget that Scotch whisky recently accounted for around a quarter of the UK's total food and drink exports! With as many people with Scottish heritage living in the US as there are in Scotland its influence continues to shape the world. Scotland's culture is enriched as much its 790 beautiful islands as it is by its stunning highlands and vibrant cities. In this book, we look at the history, mythology and dialect which has evolved in different parts of the country.

iStock

Were you aware that Edinburgh was the first city in the world to have its own fire brigade? Did you know that Scotland is home to the world's tallest hedge? You may also be surprised to hear that the small Scottish town of Bonnybridge has become the UFO capital of the world, with more than 300 sightings every year!

Scotland is as closely connected with its roots as it is with its place in the modern world. Yes, it is the home of tartan, clans, caber tossing and of course golf. But it is also a country that has indisputably shaped the way many of us live today. After all, it was local man JOHN LOGIE BAIRD who created the world's first TV picture in 1925 and another local, ALEXANDER GRAHAM BELL, who invented the telephone in February 1876. The world would be a very different place without their contributions.

With so much to offer and such a strong sense of identity, it's not surprising that Scottish independence is a hot topic. Whatever happens with that, there is no doubt that Scotland's future is bright. There is so much of interest in Scotland's lowlands, highlands and islands that, sadly, we can't explore everything in this little book. But we hope that it provides a flavour of what makes Scotland such an enduringly interesting place.

Old and Young Tom Morris By Thomas Rodger

Words & Phrases

Ah'm up to high doh – I am very anxious and at the end of my tether

A pint and a hauf – a pint of beer and a glass of whisky (chaser)

Auld Reekie – Edinburgh

Awa' an' bile yer heid! – Get lost, I have no time for you! (Literally: *'Away and boil your head'*)

In the name of the wee man! – Goodness me!

It's a sair fecht – It's a hard life

Lang may yer lum reek – I wish you prosperity and a long life (literally: *'Long may your chimney smoke'*)

Scotch – Only use this when referring to whisky, eggs, and mist – never people!

Wee dram – A glass of whisky

Ye'll get yer heid in yer hauns to play with – You'll be in serious trouble (Literally: *'You will get your head in your hands to play with'*)

Bagpipes

'Did ye no hear aboot the piper that lived up a close in the New Toon?'
'Naw, Ah dinnae ken aboot that.'
'The neighbours complained aboot the racket so he took aff his shoes!'

iStock

Glossary

The words are coded **Doric** (D), **Dundee** (Dun), **Glaswegian** (G), **Orcadian** (O) and **Shetlandic** (S). There are no codes after words that are in general use in Scotland. Some Gaelic words are included although this is a language and not a dialect.

A

Aberdeen – Aibirdeen (Dun)
Above – abeen (D), abuin (O), abune
Apple core – dump (G), casket, stump

B

Bad-tempered – crabbit
Beach – ayre (O) (S), traigh (Gaelic)
Beautiful – bonnie
Bed – scratcher (G), böl (S)
Beetle – gablo (O), hundiclock (S), bittle
Be quiet – wheesht (G), shoosh (G) hadd dee tongue (S), had yir wheest (O)

C

Cold – caul (D), Baltic (G), atteri (S), cawld (O), Bahltic (Dun), cald (Dun)
Cough – hosst (O), crim (S), hauch
Cupboard (built-in) – press (Dun) (G), aumrie (O)
Cup of tea – fly (D), cuppa (G)

D

Dagger – biodag (D), dirk
Dead – away a place (G), deid (O), deed

E

Every – ilka (D)
Exhausted – forfauchan (D), trachied (D), deeskit (O), disjaskit (S), wabbit (G), laid by (S)
Eyes – een (S)

F

Fairy – trow (S), hill-trow (O)
Farm – garth (O), ferm (O)
Father – faider (S), Da (G), faether (O)
Ferry – aiseag (Gaelic)
Few – puckle (D), twartree (S), twa (O)

G

Ghost – bogle (D), bawkie (O), wraith

Girl – quine (D), tittie (S), lassie (G), lass (O)

Glaswegian – Weegie

Go – geng (S), gae (Dun), gae (O)

Go-cart – bogie (G), piler (Dun)

Children playing on Go-Cart – CC

Going – gyaun (D), gawn (G), gyung (O)

Good – braw (G), rerr (G), göd (S) guid (O)

Goodbye – mar sin leibh (Gaelic), cheerio (G)

Grandfather – aald daa (S), granda (G), daa (O)

Grandmother – minnie (S), nana (G), grannie

H

Hailstones – haily-puckles (S), hailstaines (G), hailie-puckles (O)

Halfpenny – bawbee (D), haufpenny (G), maik (Dun)

Happy, pleased – blide (O), chuffed (G), canty (S)

Harbour – acarsaid (Gaelic)

M

Man – min (D) (Dun), Jimmy (G), man-buddie (O)

Meal, food – bursten (S), tea (dinner) (G), scran (G), maet (O)

Mess – sotter (D), aggle (O), clashnmelt (S), murgadge (S), midden (G), plester (O)

Midge – mudjo (O), mudjick (S), midgie (G), mijee (Dun)

Moan, whine, complain – weh (O), maen (S), girn (G)

P

Paper bag – poke (G)

Pencil – calafine (S), pinsil (Dun)

Pillow – cod (O), puhlae (Dun), pilla (G)

Poison – pooshan (D), pooshon (O), pushion (G)

Porridge – gruel (S), groal (O), doing time in the Bar L (G), Brose (G)

Potatoes (mashed) – shappit tatties(S), bashed tatties (G), chappid tatties (O), champit tatties

R

Rabbit – moppie (O), kyunnen (S), bunny (G)

Rain (fine) – dagg (O), driv (O), drizzle (G), raag (S), smirr, muggrofu (rain with mist) (O)

Rain (heavy downpour) – rashan (O), lashin' (G), tömald (S), stoatin' (G), teemin' (G) vaanloop (S), poorin (Dun), ootfa (O), peltin' (G)

S

Snowstorm – blindroo (O), mell-moorie (S)

Stay, staying – bide (D) (O) (Dun), bade, stiy (Dun)

Smoke (fire) – rikk (D), rook (S), reek

Suspect – jalouse (D) (S) (O), dreed(S)

Swollen, swelling – heuved (O), hivvet (S)

T

Tell-tale – clashpie (S), clipe (D) (G) (O), clash-pie (O)

Thank you – cheers (G), ta

Then – syne (D), be dat (S), than (O)

Thumb – toom (S) (O)

Tired – waabit (D), ootdön (S), wabbit (G), puggled (O)

Tooth – yackle (molar) (S) (O), teeth (O)

Proverbs from the Kingdom of Fife

Fareweel, Bonnie Scotland, Ah'm awa' tae Fife!

A deaf man will hear the clink o' money.

Choose yer wife wi' her nightcap on.

Harbour-side Warehouse in Lerwick
Shetland Islands - iStock

Orkney and Shetland Islands

Shetlandic is the dialect of the Shetland Isles and is said to come from the dialect brought to the islands by the lowland Scots from Fife and the Lothians, influenced by the Scandinavians. Old Norse, called *Norn*, used to be spoken in Orkney, Shetland and Caithness, but after Norway pledged these islands to the Scots in the 15th century the Norn language eventually became dominant. The Orcadian dialect spoken in Orkney still has remnants of Norse words and is considered soft and musical. Due to these islands' historic links with Norway, Gaelic is not spoken here.

Orkney and Shetland are not two islands but archipelagos. Orkney has 67 islands with about 16 of them inhabited and they lie off the coast of Caithness. North Ronaldsay is the most northern island: Shetland is around 56 miles (90km) further north from here and it is about the same distance to Cape Farewell in Greenland. Shetland consists of over 100 islands with only 15 of them being inhabited. It is around a hundred miles (145 km) from Fair Isle to Out Stack, the most northerly point of Britain.

An Orcadian riddle

Foweer hing-hangers,
An' foweer ching-changers,
An' een comes dinglan efter
An English version
Four hang, four walk,
Four stand skyward,
And one comes shaking behind

The answer is a cow with its four teats, four legs and a tail.

An Orkney tongue twister

This is from The Orkney Dictionary – recommended reading and available from the Orcadian Bookshop.

Whither wid yi rather
Ur rather wid yi wjither
Hiv a stewed soo's snoot
Ur a soo's snoot stewed?

The Road to the Isles (traditional Hebridean song)

The far Cuillins are pullin' me away,
As take I wi' my crummack to the road,
The far Cuillins are putting love on me,
As step I wi' the sunlight for my load.
Sure by Tummel and Lock Rannoch and Lochaber I will go.
By heather tracks wi' heaven in their wiles.

Highland Cattle with the Cuillins in the background - iStock

If it's thinkin' in your inner heart, the
braggart's in my step,
You've never smelt the tangle o' the
Isles.

Glesga Patter

Ah'm urnae gonnae hurt ye! – I'm not going to hurt you (*'so long as ye do wit Ah tell ye …'*)

Are ye right? – Are you ready?

C'moan on, get aff! – This is where you get off the bus

Eh, no? – Isn't that right?

Fish supper – Fish and chips. Chippies also sell pie suppers, haggis suppers etc.

Geeza slug o' yer ginger – Give me a drink from your bottle of lemonade

Gie it laldie, 'Ye cannae shuv yer grannie aff a bus…' – Sing lustily, *'You cannot push your granny off the bus…'*

Glesga kiss – Head-butt

Gonnae geeza a haun? – Please help me

Gonnae no dae that – Don't do that

How's it gaun? – How are you?

Jammy piece – Jam sandwich

Jings, Ma, that dug's hoachin'! – Heavens above, Mother, that dog has lots of fleas!

Ma heid's loupin' so it is. How's that? Ah dinna ken but mibbe a wee whisky 'ill sort it oot – I have a headache. Why is that? I don't know but perhaps a small whisky is the answer.

Nae bother at aw – No problem

Shoot the craw! – Make a quick exit

The Subway or Clockwork Orange – Glasgow's underground railway system

They've gan doon the watter fur the Fair – They have gone to a seaside resort by sailing down the Clyde from the Broomielaw for the Fair Fortnight (when the factories used to close for two weeks in July)

Ya beauty! or Ya dancer! – Fantastic!

Ye ken fine well that … – Don't deny it, you know that…

LEGENDS & Folklore

FAIRIES

In Scotland there were a number of names for fairies and they were said to appear in many forms.

Broadly speaking they were separated into two groups – the **Seelie Court**, who were graceful, often aristocratic and generally well disposed towards humanity, and the **Unseelie**, who were grotesque and usually malevolent. Seelie means 'blessed'. The Seelie would always repay a kindness, often with considerable generosity. After a poor woman in the Highlands gave a fairy a quantity of meal, even though she had barely enough to eat herself, she found that her meal-bin remained topped up throughout the following winter. Other poor people favoured by the fairies for their cleanliness and good manners might be presented with gifts of bread and corn during lean periods.

A number of people claimed to be on excellent terms with the Seelie Court. The most interesting was ROBERT KIRK, the minister of Aberfoyle, a pretty village in the Trossachs, during the 17th century. In 1691 he wrote a fascinating book called *The Secret Commonwealth of Elves, Fauns and Fairies*. As a native of the village, a trusted clergyman and a speaker of the Gaelic language, Kirk was uniquely placed to record the beliefs and folklore that were fast disappearing from even remote corners of the British Isles during the 1600s. Increasingly repressive forms of Protestantism and the rise of a scientific orthodoxy combined to erode cultural beliefs that had been cherished for centuries. People like Kirk were determined to preserve them while there was still time.

The church at Aberfoyle. A former minister of the village is rumoured to have been captured by fairies after becoming too curious about them - iStock

However, *The Secret Commonwealth* is more than just a collection of folk beliefs held by his neighbours. Kirk gives every impression of believing in fairies himself. For him, they were spirits inhabiting a world close to our own but distinct from it. A year after he wrote his book (which wasn't, in fact, published until the 19th century), Kirk died. His body was found lying on the *Fairy Knowe*, a large mound behind the church. The local Seelie Court was thought to lie beneath the Fairy Knowe, hence its name, and rumour spread that Kirk was not in fact dead, but had been captured by the fairies in revenge for his writing about them and giving away their secrets.

Sea Fairies

In addition to the Seelie and Unseelie courts, Scottish folklore is rich in stories of fairies who lived in the sea. Not surprisingly, these traditions were most strong in Orkney, Shetland and the Hebrides. The best-known order of Scottish sea-going fairies were the **'Selkies'**, who were believed to live as seals in the sea but who would shed their skins on dry land and become humanoid. They were also known as **'the Roane'**.

The male selkies were said to be devastatingly handsome and possessed of an animal magnetism mortal women found hard to resist. The lonesome wives of fishermen who spent months on end at sea were especially vulnerable to their charms.

Sometimes the selkie didn't need to make any of the running: a lonely or disappointed woman seeking a selkie husband only needed to weep seven tears into the sea to summon one.

Mermaids and mermen also feature in Scottish lore and were the archetypal half-human, half-fish creatures found in folklore everywhere. In Scotland, however, it was believed they were unable to come onto land and could survive out of water no longer than a fish could.

The Baobhan Sith

(pronounced *'bavan shee'*) was a species of vampire which haunted the wild Highlands. In one tale, four young men out hunting on the moors in Wester Ross met with an unpleasant fate. At nightfall they took shelter in a sheep-hut and one of them said he wished for female company to dance with. The others sighed in agreement – and then four young women suddenly sauntered through the door. One of the delighted men played the jew's harp while the others danced. As they circled round the little hut, the musician noticed that blood was dripping from his friends, and the fourth girl was approaching him with a hungry look in her eyes.

The young man ran out of the hut, pursued by the shrieking Baobhan Sith. He got among the horses, which somehow protected him, but the vampire prowled round and round him all night. She vanished at dawn. When the boy went to check on his friends, he found them lifeless on the ground, the blood drained from their bodies.

THE SCENTS OF CULLODEN

Culloden Moor is the site of the last major battle to be fought on British soil (on 16 April 1746) and is certainly one of the most haunted battlegrounds. Phantom soldiers have been seen on the anniversary of the battle, in which the Jacobite forces of BONNIE PRINCE CHARLIE were defeated by an army under the command of the DUKE OF CUMBERLAND.

Strange lights and the sounds of battle have also been reported and one man claimed to have seen a vision of the opposing armies in the sky above the field as he looked out of the window of a passing train. There is also said to be the ghost of a Highlander who mutters the word *'Defeated'* before vanishing before the eyes of startled witnesses. St. Mary's Well on the battlefield is also said to be haunted by the ghosts of Jacobites.

One visitor to the battlefield related how she had noticed that a square of Stuart tartan cloth had been blown down from a memorial stone and onto a grave. She picked it up, intending to replace it, only to see lying beneath it the prone body of a handsome young Highlander. Realising she was witnessing something uncanny, she fled the field.

Arguably the strangest phenomenon connected to Culloden is the *'Scents'*, as highlighted in a booklet published by the Edinburgh Psychic College in the 1940s. A member of the college reproduced a letter she had received about mysterious aromas detected on the moor. The anonymity of the witness was retained. She wrote:

'Ten years ago [around 1937], my sister and I were staying in Inverness, and went to Culloden Moor … Presently, I caught the scent of roses or sweet peas or other flowers, but there was nothing to account for the scent, no flowers anywhere. Next I could smell incense, and last of all a smell of burning wood.

'In spite of looking everywhere, and in every direction, there was no sign of anything whatsoever to account for the scents. I was puzzled. Next day, I crossed to Skye, and not long afterwards I picked

up a very old magazine, left lying about by another guest. In turning the leaves I was petrified with amazement to read an article entitled 'The Scents of Culloden Moor'. The writer mentions the scent of flowers, of burning pastilles (incense).'

One of the memorials on the Battlefield of Culloden. Many people have had spooky experiences on Culloden Moor - iStock

Humour

'Of all the small nations of this earth, perhaps only the ancient Greeks surpass the Scots in their contribution to mankind.'

WINSTON CHURCHILL

A party of Englishmen were climbing in the Grampians. After several hours they became hopelessly lost. One of them studied the map for some time, turning it this way and that, up and down, identifying distant landmarks, consulting his compass, noting the direction of the sun. Finally he said, *'OK, you see that big mountain over there? Ben Nevis?'*

'Yes,' answered the others eagerly.

'Well, according to the map, we're standing on top of it.'

'The Glasgow invention of square-toed shoes was to enable the Glasgow man to get closer to the bar.' *Jack House, aka Mr Glasgow*

A Shetland farmer's wife, who was rather stingy with her whisky, was giving her shepherd a drink. As she handed him his glass, she said, *'This is an especially good drop of whisky; it's fourteen years old.'*

'Aye, mistress,' said the shepherd, regarding his glass sorrowfully. *'It's very small for its age.'*

Ewan decided to call his father-in-law *'The Exorcist'* because every time he came to visit he made the spirits disappear.

Winters can be extremely cold in northern Scotland, so the new owner of the Aberchalder estate felt he was doing a good deed when he bought earmuffs for his gamekeeper, Archie. Noticing, however, that Archie wasn't wearing the earmuffs even on the coldest day, the owner asked, *'Didn't you like the earmuffs I gave you, Archie?'* Not wishing to upset his employer, Archie replied, *'Och, they are a wondrous thing.'*

'Then why don't you wear them?' asked his guv'nor.

'Well, I wore them the first day,' Archie explained, *'but at lunchtime somebody offered to buy me a drink and I didnae hear him.'*

At an antiques auction in Edinburgh, a wealthy American announced that he had lost his wallet containing £10,000. *'I'll give a reward of £100 to the guy who finds it,'* he said.

From the back of the hall, a Scottish voice shouted, *'I'll give £150!'*

One day, old Duncan bought a bottle of fine whisky and was carrying it home when he slipped on the icy road and came a cropper. As he got up, he felt something wet on his trousers. He looked up to the heavens and said, *'Oh Lord, please, I beg you let it be blood!'*

An old soldier was reminiscing to his grandchildren about his wartime experiences with the Gordon Highlanders. *'Yes, I fought in Africa, Italy and Germany. I fought with Montgomery, I fought with Wavell and I fought with Alexander.'*

His granddaughter looked up and said, *'Couldn't you get on with anybody, Grandad?'*

Jack finds himself in dire trouble. He's already lost his business and is having yet more serious financial problems. He's so desperate that he decides to ask God for help. *'God, please help me. Ah've lost ma wee store and if Ah dinna get some money, Ah'm going to lose my hoose too. Please let me win the lottery!'*

Lottery night comes and goes. Someone else wins. Jack prays again. *'God, please let me win the lottery! Ah've lost my wee store, ma hoose and Ah'm going to lose ma car as weel!'*

Lottery night comes and goes again! Still no luck... Jack prays again. *'Ah've lost ma business, ma hoose and ma car. Ma bairns are starving. Ah dinna often ask Ye for help and Ah have always been a good servant to Ye. PLEASE just let me win the lottery this one time so Ah can get back on ma feet!'*

Suddenly there is a blinding flash as the heavens open and the voice of God Himself thunders, *'Jack, at least meet me halfway, man, and buy a ticket!'*

....

Seen on a poster in Crieff: DRINK IS YOUR ENEMY.
Someone had graffitied on it: LOVE THINE ENEMY.

....

A very popular man dies in Glasgow and his old widow wishes to tell all his friends at once so she goes to the newspaper and says, *'I'd like tae place an obituary fur ma late husband.'*

The man at the desk says, *'OK, how much money dae ye have?'*

The old woman holds out a crumpled £5 note.

'You won't get many words for that, hen, but write something and we'll see.'

The woman writes down: *Peter Reid, fae Parkheid, deid* and hands it over to the man.

'Och, ye can have a few more words, hen,' he says, feeling a bit sorry for the poor old woman.

She ponders for a moment then writes some more and hands the paper back. The man reads it: *Peter Reid, fae Parkheid, deid. Ford Focus for sale.*

....

An American lady visitor cornered an Argyle man at the Highland Games ground. *'Gee! I've heard about you Scotch guys and your kilts,'* she said, *'Do you mind telling me what's worn under your kilt?'*

'*Nothing is worn under the kilt, madam,*' said the Argyle man proudly. '*Everything is as good as new.*'

....

Alisdair Biggar, from Auchtermuchty, was being interviewed for the New York Police Department. The inspector glared at him and asked, '*How would you disperse a large, unruly crowd?*'

'*Well,*' replied Alisdair thoughtfully, '*I'm no too sure how ye do it here in New York, but in Aberdeen we just pass the hat aroond, and they soon begin to shuffle off.*'

....

Willie was having his appendix out and was driving the doctor mad with questions.

'*Will Ah be able to play the bagpipes after ma operation?*' he asked.

'*Of course you will,*' snapped the doctor.

'*That's amazing!*' marvelled Willie. '*Ah couldna play them before!*'

....

A man on a South Western Line train going from Stranraer to Glasgow is very tired and hungover so he spends most of the journey dozing. After some time, he wakes up with a jolt, feeling a little disoriented. There are two old Glaswegian ladies in the compartment with him and he asks one, '*Do you know if I've passed Ayr yet?*'

'*Two or three times, young man,*' she replied, '*but we opened the compartment window.*'

....

An American tourist went out driving in Kirkcudbrightshire and on the way home he asked a local farmer for directions.

'*Excuse me, dude, could you possibly tell me the quickest way to London?*'

'*Are ye driving or walking, laddie?*' asked the farmer.

'*Driving,*' the American replied.

The farmer nodded. '*Aye, that's definitely the quickest way.*'

Ghost Stories

TALES OF THE SUPERNATURAL TO CHILL THE BLOOD

EDINBURGH

Scotland's capital is almost unrivalled for the number of haunted sites it can offer. Only London can dispute its title of the most haunted city in Britain.

But no city has made more of its haunted heritage than Edinburgh. There are at least two tourist attractions whose main appeal is the ghosts allegedly haunting them.

The best known of these is **The Real Mary King's Close**. Mary King's Close is a rare survivor of medieval Edinburgh, a narrow street which was shut off during an outbreak of plague in the 17th century and afterwards buried and therefore preserved beneath subsequent buildings. Shut off from the modern world, as well as a place where many people died in squalor, it is undeniably creepy. Other than the possible spirit of a small girl (for whom tourists still leave gifts), the Close's haunted reputation today rests largely on the feelings of unease experienced by hundreds of visitors every year and by the 'orbs' and odd 'mists' and other light anomalies picked up on cameras.

Nonetheless, paranormal activity was first reported here centuries ago. MR

THOMAS COLTHEART was one of the few people to risk moving back into Mary King's Close after the plague had subsided and he found the now-enclosed area had become badly haunted. He claimed he and his family became the victims of considerable disturbance, unsettling poltergeist activity and the startling appearance of disembodied hands and heads. In a weird twist of fate, Coltheart himself became a ghost: his form was seen by a number of witnesses after his death.

The **Niddry Street Vaults** is another very spooky place, historically interesting but now heavily marketed for its haunted reputation. The Vaults consists of an entirely enclosed series of chambers within a city bridge. They were rediscovered in the 1980s. Scores of people died in a fire in the Vaults in 1824 and this may have inspired the phenomena which became known 'the South Bridge Poltergeist' in the following decades.

After the Vaults reopened as a tourist attraction in 1996, more spooky activity was reported. The various presences and apparitions are of uncertain identity and include 'the Watcher', a solitary, silent apparition of a man in a long cloak. An invisible force, which pushes and shoves visitors, is said to exist in one chamber and in another a gang of burly builders fled in a panic after being pelted with stones and seeing their equipment being moved about. DR RICHARD WISEMAN of the University of Hertfordshire ran an investigation here, monitoring the experiences of volunteers spending hours on their own in separate vaults. One heard breathing and another saw a figure wearing an apron. Variations in magnetic fields and air movements were recorded from the 'haunted' chambers.

Edinburgh is one of Europe's most exciting and historical cities. Its haunted heritage too is arguably second to none - iStock

The most 'touristy' part of Edinburgh is the **Royal Mile**, a series of streets that run from the castle eastwards to **Holyrood Palace** for a distance of about a Scots mile, a defunct unit of measure which was about three hundred yards longer than an English mile. A walk down the Royal Mile passes many of Edinburgh's haunted sites.

An extraordinary number of ghosts are claimed for **Edinburgh Castle.** A phantom drummer boy is believed to patrol the battlements, thumping out a loud tattoo as a warning of coming calamity. The apparition of a former prisoner also haunts the battlements, where he died centuries ago in a reckless bid for freedom. The ghost of JANET DOUGLAS, Lady of Glamis, who was executed here in the 16th century for conspiracy to murder KING JAMES V, wanders in various parts of the castle. A ghostly dog has been seen in the area of the old pets' cemetery and spectral cats have been observed in one of the houses within the castle walls. The sound of a galloping horse has been heard late at night thundering over the bridge and past the guardroom.

GLASGOW

Scotland's largest city also has its fair share of ghosts. The apparition of two men in 18th-century costume has been seen in the vicinity of **George Street**. They are a cheerful pair, strolling along and chatting amicably – although silently – to each other. They were seen by a shift-worker returning home in the small hours of the morning. They ambled along beside him for a while, exchanging their silent gossip, and then, in the wink of an eye, vanished.

The creepiest location in Glasgow is its **Necropolis**, an extensive cemetery distinguished by ornate Gothic tombs of the 19th century.

Actually there are two cemeteries. **The Southern Necropolis** is in **the Gorbals**. Several odd stories are told about the Southern Necropolis. According to organisers of ghost walks here, a statue on the memorial to the innocuously named *Mrs Smith* has a habit of turning its head to stare at passers-by! Even stranger is the incident which took place in the 1960s, when gangs of Gorbals kids invaded the cemetery in search of a vampire. This was no ordinary vampire (if there is such a thing): this one had metal fangs. The youngsters were so convinced of the existence of this monster and its predations on local schoolchildren that they formed a posse, armed themselves with stakes, and set off to dispatch it. The police had to be called to calm the situation. It is thought a pulp horror comic may have inspired the belief in the **Vampire with Iron Teeth**.

GHOSTS IN THE WILD

According to the Historic Scotland website, it was at **Jedburgh Abbey**, a grand ecclesiastical ruin in the Borders, that a terrifying spectre prophesied doom to KING ALEXANDER III. In 1285 Alexander married his second queen, YOLANDE DE DREAUX, in the abbey church and it was here, say Historic Scotland, that a spirit suddenly manifested among the congregation and warned the king that he would die in the coming year. The prophecy came true when, some months later, Alexander's horse panicked in a storm and threw him over a cliff. Other authorities place this event at the castle at Jedburgh during the wedding feast. In a scene which may have inspired EDGAR ALLAN POE'S *The Masque of the Red Death*, a figure dressed in a shroud made its solemn way through the crowds of merrymakers, casting a pall, as it were, on the party.

Jedburgh Abbey - iStock

The furious king ordered his guards to grab the intruder, but to their horror and dismay they found the grave-clothes 'untenanted by any tangible form'. The grim figure, thus unmolested, continued its procession to the throne. It stood before the king, pointed to him, and vanished.

Far and away the strangest of the wild places of Scotland – stranger even than **Loch Ness** – is **Ben Macdui**, the highest mountain in the Cairngorms and the second highest in Scotland. It is popular with climbers, many of whom have reported peculiar experiences on its summit and the approaches. A booklet called *The Grey Man of Ben Macdhui and Other Abnormal Happenings*, published by the Edinburgh Psychic College in 1949, first brought the phenomena to the public's attention and much has been written about them since then.

The most commonly reported phenomenon is the sound of footsteps stomping along behind climbers and walkers on the otherwise empty mountain. A number of professional climbers as well as experienced amateurs, including a Professor of Organic Chemistry and a botanist from the University of Aberdeen, are among those who have heard the eerie footfalls. The cairn on the summit is one of the focal points of these sounds and it has been suggested they are made by the contracting and expansion of stones in the cold mountain air. However, the phenomenon seems too dramatic for such a simple explanation. And the crunching of footsteps is not the only inexplicable noise to have troubled people on Ben Macdui. Unearthly music has also been heard and also 'an enormously resonant Gaelic-speaking voice'.

On rare occasions the being supposed to be making the mysterious footsteps has been glimpsed. Known as the

Big Grey Man, it is described it as a gigantic shadowy figure in the mist. In this it resembles the entirely natural phenomenon of the *'Spectre of the Brocken'* (named after an Alpine peak), caused when a climber's shadow is projected onto a bank of cloud by low sun. However, most mountaineers would be familiar with this effect. A few people have got a closer look at the *Grey Man* but their descriptions all vary, from *'a tall, stately human figure'* to an apelike *'great brown creature'* and a demonic entity *'with pointy ears, long legs and feet with talons'*.

The summit of Ben Macdui is remote and inaccessible, only to be attempted by well-equipped and experienced fellwalkers and mountaineers. It is unwise to attempt the summit alone, not only for the obvious reasons of mountain safety but also because the mysterious entity known as the *Big Grey Man* is still decidedly active, and he has been both seen and heard in recent years. The risk of encountering a gigantic phantom in the mist and then finding oneself running off a cliff in uncontrollable fright seems too much for even the most daring ghost hunter!

The summit of Ben Macdhui in the Cairngorms, home of the terrifying phantom known as 'The Big Grey Man' – CC

Scottish *Recipes*

AUTHOR: AMANDA WRAGG

Oatcakes

These tasty biscuits (or bannocks) are so Scottish they're positively tartan. Easy to make, they're perfect with farmhouse cheese and good chutney. And the smell in the kitchen when you're making them is worth the effort alone. You can use rolled oats, but pinhead oatmeal will produce the real deal.

INGREDIENTS:

225g plain flour

½ tsp baking powder

50g chilled butter

1 tsp salt

½ tsp granulated sugar

70ml hot water

Oatcakes - iStock

Method

Pre-heat the oven to 190°C/Gas 5. In a large bowl mix together the oatmeal, flour, sugar and baking powder. Cut the chilled butter into small pieces and add to the flour. Rub together until you have the consistency of breadcrumbs.

Add the water bit by bit and combine until you've got a thick dough. Sprinkle some extra flour on a work surface and roll the dough out – about half a centimetre thick. Use a cookie cutter to make shapes.

Place the oatcakes on a baking tray and bake for about 20 minutes until golden brown. I defy you to wait until they've cooled down before you're spreading one with butter…

Fisherman's Pie - iStock

Fisherman's Pie

There's nowhere in Scotland more than 50 miles from the sea so fresh fish has always been central to the Scottish diet. This simple, family-friendly recipe calls for white and smoked fish

– and if you're feeling flush, a handful of large prawns elevates it to a dinner party cracker. One of the great things about this recipe is that you don't have to cook the fish before you build the dish. The jury's out on whether or not grated cheese goes on top; it's entirely up to you, and no one's judging you.

INGREDIENTS (serves 4)

1 tbsp olive oil

1 leek, thinly sliced*

30g flour

300ml milk

125g prawns

Sea salt

Freshly ground black pepper

60g smoked haddock fillets

60g white fish

3 large potatoes, peeled and thinly sliced

METHOD

Pre-heat the oven to 200°C/Gas 6. Heat the oil over a medium heat. Add the leeks and fry for 2–3 minutes, until soft but not brown. Add the flour, stir well and cook for 1–2 minutes.

Remove the pan from the heat and gradually stir in the milk. Return to the heat and cook, stirring constantly until the sauce thickens. Simmer gently for five minutes.

Stir in the prawns and season well with salt and pepper. Place half the sauce in the pie dish. Place the fish fillets on top then spoon over the remaining sauce. Top with the sliced potato and season some more.

Place the dish on a baking sheet and bake for 35–40 minutes, until the potatoes are golden.

Serve with garden peas, broad beans or mange tout.

*a foolproof way to make sure you've got all the grit out between the layers of leek is to put them into cold salted water for 10 minutes.

Tweed Kettle

iStock

A deeply traditional Scottish dish, this is sometimes called salmon hash and graced dining tables in the 19th century. A classic dish of salmon with white wine and shallot sauce it's quite sophisticated and goes down a storm at dinner parties. The Tweed is one of Scotland's premier salmon rivers and though this dish originates in Edinburgh it's been named in its honour.

INGREDIENTS (serves 4)

900g fresh salmon

2 chopped shallots

Sea salt

Freshly ground black pepper

150ml water

150ml dry white wine

2 tbsp butter

115g mushrooms, chopped

Pinch of ground mace

1 tbsp flat leaf parsley

METHOD

Put the fish in a large pan (if you've got a fish kettle, this is the time to dust it down) just covered with water, and bring to the boil. Simmer gently for five minutes. Remove fish from the pan, keeping the stock; remove skin and bone and cut the fish into bite-size squares.

Season with salt, pepper and mace and put into a clean dish with a quarter pint of the fish stock plus the wine and finely chopped shallot or chives. Cover the dish and simmer gently for about 20 minutes.

Heat up the butter and soften the mushrooms in it, drain and add to the salmon and heat together for another five minutes. Serve with chopped parsley. Traditionally this dish is served with mashed swede or potatoes.

Scottish Beef Casserole with Dumplings

iStock

Scotland produces some of the best beef in the world; ABERDEEN ANGUS is arguably the best-known breed, renowned for the rich and tasty flavour of the meat. Everyone has their own version of this classic dish; a long, slow cook brings the taste out of all the component parts of this rib-sticking winter warmer. Beer-wise, there are dozens of large and micro-breweries up and down the country; choose any dark, sweet variety here.

INGREDIENTS (serves 4 to 6)

1 tbsp sunflower oil

750g beef shin, stewing steak or skirt, diced

4 small onions, peeled and diced

4 carrots, peeled and diced

2 celery stalks, diced

3 bay leaves

2 tbsp Worcestershire Sauce

500ml bottle beer

Sea salt and freshly ground black pepper

FOR THE DUMPLINGS

175g self-raising flour

75g shredded suet

Salt & pepper

1 tsp dried thyme

Cold water

METHOD

Warm the oil in a large casserole pot. Add the meat and let it brown slightly, then remove and keep warm. Add the onions and cook until they're transparent but not brown; add the rest of the vegetables and sweat for 5 minutes. Put the meat back then add the beer, tomatoes, Worcestershire Sauce, bay leaves and seasoning. Put the lid on and simmer for about 1½ hours

FOR THE DUMPLINGS

Sift the flour into a bowl then add the suet, seasoning and thyme. Add about 5 tbsp cold water, and mix together till you have a soft, slightly sticky dough. Flour your hands and put the dough on a floured surface. Shape the dough into a big ball then cut up into about 8 balls. Drop the dumplings into the stew and cook with the lid off for a further 15 minutes until they're plump and moist.

Serve straight from the pot with crusty bread to soak up the gravy!

Cranachan

iStock

This seriously boozy dessert is a traditional Scottish dish and a great alternative to trifle. It's really simple to make (no actual cooking) and absolutely delicious – your dinner guests will be impressed!

INGREDIENTS (serves 4)

550ml double cream

85g porridge oats

7 tbsp whisky

3 tbsp runny honey

450g raspberries or strawberries

Fresh mint, to garnish

METHOD

Toast the oats in a frying pan. Lightly whip the cream until it stands in soft peaks then fold in the whisky, honey, oatmeal and berries.

Serve in dessert glasses garnished with a few berries and mint leaves.

Colcannon

This hearty, economical dish originated in Ireland but it's been eaten the length and breadth of Scotland for centuries; in the Borders it's known as Rumbledethumps and in Aberdeenshire as Kailkenny. There are several variations include adding a couple of boiled and mashed carrots and turnips, and sometimes cream is used instead of butter. Regardless of which additions you choose you can be sure that the family will rush to the table and polish off the lot.

INGREDIENTS

450g potatoes

450 cabbage

30g butter

Sea salt and freshly ground black pepper

METHOD

Boil and mash the potatoes. Boil the cabbage then finely chop it. Mix in a large saucepan in which the butter has been melted. Keep the saucepan over a low heat to keep it hot. Season to taste and serve piping hot.

The mixture can also be put into a greased oven-proof dish and cooked at 200°C/Gas Mark 6 until the top is browned.

iStock

Famous *Locals*

SIR ALEX FERGUSON was born in Glasgow in December 1941 and brought up in Govan. He became one of the most successful football managers in Britain, winning 49 trophies with St Mirren, Aberdeen and Manchester United. He retired as a football manager at Manchester United in 2013 but remained at the club as a director. A statue of Sir Alex, designed by Scottish sculptor Philip Jackson, was unveiled at Manchester United's Old Trafford home in November 2012.

iStock

KATHERINE GRAINGER CBE was born in Glasgow in 1975 and attended Bearsden Academy. She has an honours Law degree from Edinburgh University, a PhD in Medical Law from Glasgow University and is a Fellow of Kings College London. She took up rowing in 1993 and is now Britain's most successful female rower. She won her first silver Olympic medal in the Women's Quad event at the Sydney Games in 2000 and since then she has won silver at both the 2004 Athens and 2008 Beijing Olympics. In the London 2012 Olympics, Grainger won her gold medal alongside Anna Watkins in the Women's Double Sculls event. Between 2003 and 2011 she won six gold medals and a silver in the Rowing World Championships.

Muriel Spark - CC

DAME MURIEL SPARK (1918–2006)

The poet and novelist was born at 160 Bruntsfield Place in Edinburgh. She attended James Gillespie's High School for Girls where she was encouraged by her teacher Christina Kay to become a writer. Indeed it was Christina who inspired the title character in Muriel's novel *The Prime of Miss Jean Brodie*, published in 1961. The novel is set in Edinburgh in the 1930s and Miss Brodie is determined to give six ten-year-old girls a wide education so she includes lessons about love, travel, art history and fascism.

A play based on the novel became a hit in London's West End and New York's Broadway and the film version, directed by RONALD NEAME in 1969, won actress MAGGIE SMITH an Oscar.

ALEXANDER GRAHAM BELL (1847–1922) was born at 14 South Charlotte Street, Edinburgh, making Edinburgh in effect the home of the telephone. His works and studies in teaching deaf people continued in London and in America, where he became a naturalised citizen in 1874. Working with his assistant THOMAS A. WATSON, Bell transmitted speech sounds using his membrane diaphragm transmitter in June 1875. A year later, after some improvements, they transmitted intelligible speech over wires. In 1880, Bell moved on to developing the photophone. While it was no use for selfies it enabled speech signals to be transmitted using a light beam powered by a selenium cell.

The house where Alexander Graham Bell was born - Katherine Buchanan

Karen Gillan

Born in Inverness in 1987, Karen Gillan shot to fame as AMY POND, companion to the eleventh Doctor in the long-running BBC sci-fi series DOCTOR WHO. In her time in the role she charmed Doctor Who fans with her energy and dry sense of humour. While that TARDIS-travelling role sadly had to end, Gillan has gone on to shine in films such as *The Circle, Not Another Happy Ending, Oculus, Guardians of the Galaxy* and *Jumanji: Welcome to the Jungle*. In 2017, Gillan wrote and directed her first feature film, *The Party's Just Beginning*.

Sir James Swinburne

Born in Inverness in the Scottish Highlands in 1858, Sir James Swinburne was a key figure in the plastics and electrical industries, so much so that he is referred to as 'the father of British plastics'. He played a vital role in bringing polyoxy-benzylmethylenglycolanhydride, or Bakelite as most of us now know it, to the market. Swinburne first became central to the electrical industry when he collaborated on creating the first electric light bulb. He was also responsible for coining the words *'stator'* and *'rotor'*. He went on to become the first President of the Institution of Electrical Engineers. Not content with this, he grew interested in plastics when introduced to a product of the phenol formaldehyde reaction. This led him to set up his company, FIREPROOF CELLULOID SYNDICATE LIMITED, to research and market the product. The company created a highly effective hard lacquer for coating metals. While he was just pipped to the post by LEO BAEKELAND in patenting synthetic resin, the two went on to work together to form the company BAKELITE LTD in 1926. Bakelite was the world's first synthetic plastic and, thanks to its ability not to conduct electricity and being heat-resistant, it became hugely popular for use in everything from firearms to toys! Today, old Bakelite items are highly sought after as collectibles.

A vintage General Electric Bakelite Table Radio – CC

SIR DOUGLAS ANDREW KILGOUR BLACK

This native of the Shetland Islands has had an enormous influence on the health and well-being of many people. The Scottish doctor and medical scientist, who was born in 1913, played a vital role in developing the National Health Service. He conducted research in the field of public health and was famous as the author of the *Black Report* on health inequalities in 1980. Black also chaired the UK government investigation into childhood leukaemia around the nuclear reprocessing plant at Sellafield, Cumbria, UK. Not surprisingly, his extensive achievements were recognised when he was created a **Knight Bachelor** in 1973 and a **Knight of the Most Venerable Order of St John of Jerusalem** in 1989.

JOSEPHINE TEY

Inverness is the birthplace of yet another Scottish person who went on to have a significant influence on culture. ELIZABETH MACKINTOSH, born in 1896, is better known by her pseudonym, Josephine Tey. This was the name under which she published her much-loved novels which include *The Daughter of Time, The Franchise Affair, Brat Farrar* and *Miss Pym Disposes*. Tey also wrote plays under the pen name GORDON DAVIOT. Her novel *A Shilling for Candles* was the basis of ALFRED HITCHCOCK'S 1937 film *Young and Innocent*.

Murder
MYSTERIES

AUTHOR: KATHRYN BUCHANAN

THE DUDSDAY MURDER

Dudsday was the name of a holiday and country fair held in Kilmarnock at which labourers and servants were hired and, according to the Ayr Advertiser, where *'country servants spend their former half year's wages on new clothes'*. It should have been a happy time but for JAMES YOUNG and his family that is not how it turned out.

James was born at Riccarton at a time when dates of birth were not always recorded, so it is thought that he was still a teenager when he met his death. His beaten body was found in Blackhill Road, near Gatehead in the parish of Dundonald in South Ayrshire, and not far from the Forty Acres where he worked for farmer Joseph Smith. His assailant was eventually proved to be JAMES McWHEELAN, who was also known as JAMES McQUEEN. He was a gardener at **Ardrossan** for a time and then worked at the **Glengarnock Iron Works**.

It appears that James Young was attacked on Friday 26 or possibly Saturday 27 May 1848 near the toll road leading from **Forty Acres Toll Bar**. It is here that the parish boundaries of Symington, Dundonald and Riccarton meet. The evidence indicates that Young was struck on the head several times with a stone or similar object, and then stabbed

Fort Acres Farm, Rosser – CC

in the neck, which resulted in him bleeding to death. It was not a quick death as his hands were clutching lumps of earth and grass as he had tried to claw his way to safety. Young's body was discovered lying in a pool of blood around four o'clock on Saturday morning by JOHN GEBBIE and JOHN SCOTT, who reported their grisly discovery to the farmer at Forty Acres and the toll keeper, ROBERT HENDRY, who were able to identify the body. Young's silver watch, chain and fifteen shillings in silver money were missing.

In some ways it is a little strange that WILLIAM ORR, a farmer, said he had been riding past the toll bar between Beith and Paisley on the Sunday when he saw McWheelan hurriedly leaving the toll house. It later transpired that 35 pounds had been stolen and it was said that Young's watch had been pawned by an acquaintance of

McWheelan. Apparently, William Orr was suspicious of McWheelan and had heard about the murder and the theft at Forty Acres Toll Bar, so he rode after McWheelan, apprehending him near Paisley and handing him over to the police.

At his trial in Ayr, McWheelan, who was described in a broadside – a sheet circulated by a printer – as being *'a good looking and stoutly built man'*, pleaded not guilty to all charges and 93 witnesses were called. The jury took only thirty minutes to find him guilty of murder and he was sentenced to death. After fifteen minutes of standing under the gallows with the rope around his neck and his head covered with a hood, McWheelan continued to pray. The hangman was uncertain when to pull the lever because James McWheelan was supposed to drop a handkerchief, in the usual fashion, to indicate he was ready. In exasperation, the Provost of Ayr shouted, *'Do your duty, executioner'*, and JOHN MURDOCH, the hangman, duly pulled the lever. McWheelan never admitted guilt and insisted upon his innocence to the last.

BURKE AND HARE

Up the close, an' doon the stair,
But an' ben wae Burke an' Hare.
Burke's the butcher; Hare's the thief,
Knox the boy that buys the beef!

(TRADITIONAL SKIPPING RHYME)

By the late 18th century, Edinburgh was well established as a city with a strong reputation for medical excellence. The university was expanding, with growing demand for places on medical degree courses, and ROBERT KNOX (1791–1862), a former army surgeon, established an anatomical school. By 1882 his lectures, which appealed to gentlemen as well as medical students, were attracting audiences of up to 500 people.

Burke and Hare - CC

To enable students and doctors to continue with their anatomical studies into the working of the human body, a continuous supply of cadavers was required. By the early 1800s, demand was outstripping supply, and although doctors were allowed to use the bodies of executed criminals and those who died in prison, the allocation to Edinburgh Medical College was only five corpses per year. This poor supply of bodies for dissection brought out the entrepreneurial skill of the 'resurrectionists', who robbed new graves knowing they could sell a fresh body for between seven and twelve pounds.

In 1827, WILLIAM BURKE, an Irish labourer, was lodging at Logue's boarding house in Tanner's Close in Edinburgh, along with his wife Helen McDougal, and it was here that he became acquainted with WILLIAM

HARE, a tall, gaunt, sly-looking man. Burke was of shorter stature and more stoutly built. When a fellow lodger, an army pensioner, died still owing back rent the two men, with their landlady MARGARET LAIRD, hit on the idea of selling the lodger's body to Dr Knox, who lived at Surgeon's Square and had a reputation of paying well for bodies brought to him for dissection – with no questions asked. To the two men and Margaret this was a sensible and logical business deal. The lodger was dead and the money paid by Dr Knox would cover the back rent owed by the deceased. Burke and Hare opened the coffin, removed the body and replaced it with weighted sacks, then resealed the coffin ready for burial.

Not long afterwards another unfortunate lodger at Tanner's Close became ill. It appeared obvious to Burke and Hare that the lodger would eventually die. They were now impatient to earn another twelve pounds after their earlier success and decided to hasten the demise of the lodger by suffocation, leaving no obvious indication of murder. Another fresh body for Dr Knox, no questions asked, and cash in hand.

Their next victim was an elderly lady, ABIGAIL SIMPSON, whom they befriended, took back to Tanner's Close and plied with alcohol. The following morning they poured more gin into the old lady until she was barely conscious and unable to resist suffocation. It is said that Dr Knox made no comment other than remarking on the fresh state of the corpse. Apparently, Burke and Hare made a profit of ten pounds, before deduction of the cost of gin. Heady with success, they next murdered a prostitute, MARY HALDANE, using the same efficient method. On one occasion, they became a little too greedy and tried to double their profit on the same night. Two women who plied their trade on the streets were invited back to Tanner's Close. MARY PATERSON cooperated by getting extremely drunk but her friend, JANET BROWN, became suspicious and left. Mary Paterson, by now senseless with alcohol, was swiftly and efficiently dispatched and taken to Dr Knox. When Mary Paterson's body was lying on Dr Knox's dissecting table there was a tricky moment when one of his students claimed to recognise her from a previous night out. However, fast talking and quick work soon rendered the body unrecognisable.

With an increasing number of victims being swiftly processed Burke and Hare and their two female partners must have relished their new-found wealth. The killings continued for ten months, and although no one knows the final total it is thought to have been about sixteen. Living and working together in close proximity proved a strain on their relationship, however, and after a dispute Burke and Helen McDougal moved out of Tanner's Close to a house close to West Port. The friendship quickly returned to normal and it was soon 'business as usual'. However, success sometimes breeds carelessness.

One of the last to die was *'Daft Jamie'*, a pleasant man and well known on the city streets. His body was also recognised when laid out on Dr Knox's table. The curtain finally came down on their activities when Burke brought home an Irishwoman called MARGARET DOCHERTY. There were other people in the house at the same time, enjoying a drinking session, and when the booze ran out the drinkers went off to buy more alcohol. While the house was empty, Burke and Hare seized the opportunity to murder Mrs Docherty. When the revellers returned they naturally enquired about the lady who had been there before, only to be told by Burke that she had decided to leave. However, it was noticed that Burke was a little edgy and insistent that no one should sit on the bed. In this party mood, and given Burke's attitude, sooner or later someone just had to look under the bed and find the body of Mrs Docherty. Burke, Hare, Laird and McDougal were arrested and committed for trial.

Hare and Laird saved their lives by turning King's Evidence, appearing as witnesses for the prosecution in Burke and McDougal's trial, which took place in December 1828. The trial lasted 24 hours, with the jury retiring to consider their verdict at 8.30am on Christmas Day. After 50 minutes' deliberation the jury found Burke guilty, and the charge against McDougal not proven. Burke was hanged at 8.15am on 28 January 1829 in torrential rain, in front of a crowd of nearly 30,000 at the Grassmarket. The Times of 2 February 1829 reported that Burke went to the gallows to *'vehement cheering from every quarter, mingled with groans and hisses'*. His body was flayed and dissected, somewhat ironically, in the Edinburgh Medical College. Burke's skeleton hangs in the museum at Surgeons' Hall, Edinburgh, and also on display is a gold-embossed pocketbook, covered with Burke's skin.

McDougal was freed after the 'not proven' verdict. Hare, as you might expect, was forced to flee Edinburgh and is believed to have ended up as a pauper on the streets of London. Robert Knox eventually found work as an anatomist at the Brompton Hospital and he died in 1862. Margaret Laird is thought to have returned to Ireland while Helen McDougal moved south to Newcastle and then County Durham, but her past always caught up with her and what happened to her in the end is unknown.

Scottish *Sports*

CURLING

There is evidence of curling being played in the 16th century at **Paisley Abbey** and **Dunblane**. **The Kilsyth Curling Club** dates back to the 1700s and is said to be the oldest in the world. Refrigeration and indoor rinks have kept curling alive whatever the weather, and it is played in Canada, America and Japan as well as Europe. Curling has been an official Olympic sport since 1998, although it had been a demonstration sport since 1924, and since then **Kays**, who are based in Mauchline in Ayrshire, have supplied the granite curling stones for the Games. Kays harvest around two thousand tons of granite every decade from **Ailsa Craig,** an island in the middle of the Firth of Clyde.

Anna Sloan – CC

SHINTY (OR CAMANACHD IN GAELIC)

It is said that shinty was introduced to the north-west of Scotland from Ireland, where hurling is still played, and *camanachd* is recorded as being played hundreds of years ago in Scotland. This sport is a cross between hockey,

University of Glasgow, the East Quadrangle of the Main Building. The University Shinty Club started 1901 - iStock

lacrosse and ice hockey, although it was being played earlier than any of those sports. Shinty was played in Scotland in the winter on special days such as festivals and New Year's Day, when villages would compete against each other, encouraged by the playing of the bagpipes and a wee dram. It was a free-for-all with as many in a team as could be mustered and no written rules.

It was not until the late 19th century that shinty became more organised and the number of players in a team was set down, as well as some other rules. The modern rules allow twelve players in each team, including a goalkeeper. The curved stick is called a *caman* and is used to strike a small leather ball with the aim of scoring goals.

Highland Games

It is possible that, originally, these games were a showcase of talents including strength, bravery and swiftness as well as Highland dancing and playing the bagpipes. The Clan Chieftain could then choose the fittest fighters, the strongest bodyguards and the best entertainers to while away the dark winter evenings. Clans would compete against each other in all of the events and many of these traditional sports can be watched today. There are small Highland Games held not very far from Edinburgh and larger events such as the Braemar Gathering, which attracts about 10,000 spectators and is always held on the first Saturday in September.

iStock

istock

Some of the sports you might see are:

Tossing the Caber: The caber is a long, heavy, trimmed tree trunk about six metres in length although the lengths do vary quite a bit. It is placed on end, the thickest end at the top. The competitor crouches down and wedges the caber between his neck and shoulder and picks it up with his hands holding the base. He tosses it so that it turns with the thick end touching the ground first. The caber should fall away from the tosser. It is not the distance that matters but the angle that the caber falls relative to the thrower.

Throwing the hammer became an event at the Highland Games in the 18th century and although similar to the modern hammer throw there are some differences. Here a round metal ball is attached to the end of a shaft about four feet (1.2 metres) in length. The hammer is swung around the head and thrown over the shoulder for the furthest possible distance.

Putting the Stone: This is similar to the shot-put but here a large stone is often used instead of a steel shot, and there are different rules on the techniques allowed to throw the stone.

The Tug o' War: This battle of strength is a big part of the Highland Games. Once used to resolve arguments, the tug o' war has been played for centuries. It was also a sport in the Summer Olympics from 1900 to 1920!

GOLF: AN AULD SCOTTISH GAME

The game of *'gowf'* was so popular in Scotland that an Act of Parliament was passed in 1457 to forbid the playing of the game on Sundays as there was concern that too much time was being spent playing golf and not enough on archery practice!

iStock

HAGGIS HURLING

With **haggis** one of Scotland's most traditional foods, you can't get a sport much more traditional than haggis hurling! Yet while many claim it is a traditional sport, haggis hurling only really gained popularity in the late 1970s when a man advertised that it would be revived at the **Gathering of the Clans** in Edinburgh. This turned out to be a joke, but the huge public response to the announcement meant that haggis hurling was here to stay. While one version of haggis hurling is enacted at festivals, the other is a professional sport and is enjoyed on an international level.

The rules of haggis hurling are very specific. The haggis must be cooked and of a certain weight, which differs for male and female contestants. The haggis hurler must stand elevated, usually on a whisky barrel, for the throw. Winning hurls are determined by distance and accuracy. In early 2017, a new record for haggis hurling was achieved at the **World Haggis Hurling Championships** at ALLOWAY, the home town of ROBERT BURNS. GARY MCLAY from Kilmarnock set a new event record by hurling a haggis to an impressive distance of 59 metres!

FITBA'

It was a Scotsman, WILLIE McGREGOR, who set up the first English football league, and the first international match was played at Partick in 1872 with the Scottish team coming entirely from Queen's Park Football Club. Before the first football clubs were formed, football was played at Glasgow Green and Queen's Park.

iStock

Local *Customs*

New Year's Eve in Edinburgh is a time for celebration. The city's Hogmanay celebrations take place over three days and start with a spectacular torchlight procession and fireworks on 30th December.

On **Hogmanay**, the city seems to be just one big street party, with concerts in Princes Street Gardens and a great atmosphere. Tens of thousands of tickets are sold to residents and visitors from around the globe every year. As the bells strike midnight, fireworks explode, lighting up the skies above Edinburgh, and the Auld Reekie partygoers sing *'Auld Lang Syne'*. When you sing *'And here's my hand…'*, cross your arms and join hands with anybody on either side of you. If it was less crowded and you were in the normal circle, you would run or stagger into the middle and out again – still holding hands!

This song has gained an international reputation and has been sung in many places around the world. An American teacher, LUTHER WHITING Mason, introduced *'Auld Lang Syne'* to the school curriculum in Japan in the 1890s and nowadays it is played there in some shops and restaurants at closing time.

Hogmanay - iStock

Burns Supper

This is a celebration of the Scottish poet, ROBERT 'RABBIE' BURNS *(1759–96)*. There is a formality to this event which has been held on his birthday, 25th January, for over 200 years, with some suppers being more strict than others. If there is a high table then the other guests are obliged to stand while the piper plays and the high table is seated. Everyone is welcomed and the *Selkirk Grace* is said before the supper:

Some hae meat and canna eat,

Some hae nane that want it,

But we hae meat and we can eat,

And sae the Lord be thankit

The haggis, carried on a silver platter, is piped in and it is usual to stand for this. The haggis is then addressed by the recitation of Burns' poem *'To a Haggis'*. The reader of the poem should have his *skean dhu* (a small dagger worn in the stocking) at the ready as when he comes to *'An cut you up wi' ready sleight'* he slices open the haggis, *'Trenching your gushing entrails bright'*. At the end of the poem there is a toast to the haggis. Supper is then

iStock

served and, traditionally, it consists of cock-a-leekie soup, haggis with bashed neeps an' champit tatties, followed by Tipsy Laird, which is a sherry trifle.

Entertainment follows and a few Burns songs are sung such as *'My Luve is Like a Red, Red, Rose'* and *'Ae Fond Kiss'*, and poems recited, the most popular being *'Tam o' Shanter'*. This is followed by a speech to the Immortal Memory of Burns, a Toast to the Lassies followed by a Reply to the Toast to the Lassies, and the evening ends with everyone singing *'Auld Lang Syne'*.

THE CHRISTENING PIECE

It was a tradition in Glasgow to give a christening piece to the first person you meet when taking a baby to be christened. If the baby is a girl then the christening piece is given to the first male and if a boy to the first female. Babies used to be christened within days of being born, but this is not always the case any more so this custom is dying out. The christening piece was made from two Abernethy biscuits or digestive biscuits spread with butter and sandwiched together with a piece of silver in between. The silver could be a silver thrupenny piece or even a half-a-crown (worth two shillings and sixpence). The biscuits would be wrapped in greaseproof paper or put in a poke (a paper bag). It was supposed to be lucky for the baby and the person who received it. Children would find out when a baby was going to be christened and they would gather outside the close, trying to be the one who was given the christening piece – maybe more for the money than for good fortune. After the christening there would be a get-together and if this was the couple's first baby, the top layer of their wedding cake would take pride of place as this had been saved to be used as the christening cake.

The Dismal Day

People who lived in the Scottish Highlands used to refuse to start anything important or special on the day on which the 3rd of March fell. This was because the day was known to them as *la Sheachanna na bleanagh*, or the **dismal day**!

Fishing Customs

Being so much at the mercy of the elements, fishing communities are well known for their superstitions. This is certainly true for fishermen in areas such as the Outer Hebrides and the East Neuk of Fife. They refused to sail if they had passed a minister on the way to their fishing boats, as it was believed to be a bad omen.

Burning the Clavie

When Britain moved over from the Julian to the Gregorian calendar in 1752, not all parts of Scotland made the change. To this day, Burghead, a small town in Morayshire, still celebrates New Year on 10th January. As part of this, the town holds a fire ceremony which is believed to have survived the Catholic Church's purge on pagan fire rituals. In the **Burning of the Clavie**, a hooped barrel, called the Clavie, is filled with old pieces of tar and wood. It is hammered onto a pole with a specially forged nail. Ten men take it in turns to carry the burning Clavie clockwise around the streets of Burghead, presenting pieces of smouldering embers to houses. These are used to keep home fires burning and the ashes are also packaged and sent by post to relatives. After the parade, the Clavie is attached to a special pillar that has been built on Doorie Hill. After yet more fuel is added, the embers are scattered down the hillside as people grab them for good luck. Having a role on the Clavie team is an honour and is passed down through families.

Local Names & Clans

Scottish Surnames

In 1016, King Malcolm III of Scotland decreed that surnames should be used, as this was the custom in other nations.

Clan chiefs adopted names from the lands that they owned, and when the king married for a second time, his new wife, MARGARET, a Saxon Princess, brought surnames to Scotland along with her entourage. These included RAMSEY, BISSET, BORTHUIK and GIFFORD. Through time, surnames also reflected trades or professions such as WARRENDER, PARKER (both of which mean 'gamekeeper') and GLOVER. After the 1745 rebellion, Gaelic names began to creep into Glasgow and were sometimes substituted for a similar-sounding name; sometimes the 'Mac' prefix, meaning 'son of', was dropped or changed to 'son', as in MACDONALD being changed to DONALDSON. MACDONALD, with a small *d*, is a patronymic surname or general surname whereas MacDonald with a capital *D* means 'the son of Donald'.

Associated with the surnames are their mottos and here are a few examples:

MACAULAY (*MacAmhlaidh* in Gaelic) means the son of Olaf and their motto '*Dulce periculum*' means '*danger is sweet*'.

COLQUHOUN (*Mac a' Chombaich* in Gaelic) is taken from the lands of Colquhoun in Dunbartonshire and their motto is '*Si je puis*', meaning '*if I can*'.

ERSKIN (*Arascain* in Gaelic) comes from the Barony of Erskine in Renfrewshire and their motto '*Je pense plus*' means '*I think more*'.

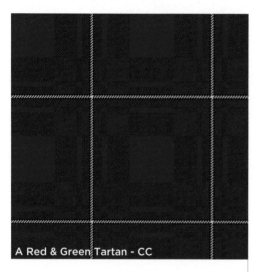
A Red & Green Tartan - CC

Clans and Tartans

Tartan is a description of how the thread is woven to make the cloth. Each thread is passed over two threads then under two threads.

The difference between a check and a tartan is that the check square shows only one colour and in tartan there are always squares when the thread colours cross. When the thread was woven into cloth it was 'waulked' by wetting, pulling, beating and stretching the tartan into shape across a wooden frame. Like many others doing jobs that demanded a rhythm to their physical labour, the workers would sing, usually in Gaelic, and here are a few translated verses of a waulking song from Carmina Gadelica by Alexander Carmichael (1832–1912):

The wool is carded, washed and dyed,
The ember heat and reeking peat
Pervade and cense the house inside,
Wall shadows in the gloom.

The threads of yellow, blue and green,
The black, the red, the white,
By fingers deft in warp and weft,
A criss-cross sett is laid between
To form the cloth aright.

The fulling at the waulking frame,
The maidens all a-row,
On either side sit well supplied,
With love-songs ready to exclaim,
In movements to and fro.

Balmoral - iStock

KING GEORGE II's Dress Act banned the wearing of Highland dress and the penalties for disobeying included deportation for seven years. Only the army could wear the kilt and the Black Watch regimental tartan. In 1822, KING GEORGE IV visited Edinburgh on the invitation of the Chair of the Celtic Society of Edinburgh, SIR WALTER SCOTT, who declared that for this special occasion *'let every man wear his tartan'*. The visit encouraged clans (families) to be identified with a particular sett (pattern) and by the end of the 1800s all the recognised clans in Scotland had their own tartans.

QUEEN VICTORIA was a supporter of Highland dress and her home at Balmoral had many tartan furnishings. There is etiquette to wearing tartan: no one outside of the Royal Family should wear the Balmoral, and chiefs' tartans should be worn only by the Chief and his immediate family. The old Hunting Stewart tartan is now regarded as a universal tartan, as are the modern *Flower of Scotland* and *Pride of Scotland* tartans.

Just as tartans reveal a great deal about Scottish identity, so do names. In the Scottish Highlands and islands, many old names still give subtle clues

iStock

to the past. For example, the name DALLAS has very different associations these days, but it is also a surname in the Highlands and islands. You can find the small village of Dallas near Elgin. It was in existence over a thousand years before its American namesake. The name comes from the Old Gaelic term *dallais* which means *'at the meadow'*. Dallases served in the MACKINTOSH regiment at the **Battle of Culloden**.

Most of us associate the surname MACBETH with *'the Scottish play'*. Made famous by SHAKESPEARE, Macbeth is probably the best-known monarch of Scotland. He ruled as king from 1040 to 1057. Shakespeare's play is so good that it can be forgiven some artistic licence. The reality was that Macbeth was *Thane of Moray* (and not *Glamis* or *Cawdor*) and the Macbeths were an established family in the north of Scotland. The name means *'son of life'* or *'son of a man of religion'*.

The distinctive name SWEENEY was originally a Highland name, *Macsuibhne*, which meant *'son of a pleasant man'*. LINKLATER is an old Orkney place name that means *'heather rock'* in Old Norse. It has been recorded as a name in the northern isles since the 15th century.

Scottish HISTORY

GLASGOW

Let Glasgow Flourish - Katherine Buchanan

Glasgow was founded by St. Mungo in the seventh century and the building of the cathedral started in 1238. Glasgow University, the second oldest in Scotland, was founded in 1451. *'Let Glasgow Flourish'* has been Glasgow's motto since 1886. It is an abridged version of the 1631 inscription on the bell of the Tron Church which declares, *'Lord, let Glasgow flourish through the preaching of thy word and the praising of thy name.'*

THE RIVER CLYDE

It is said that Glasgow made the Clyde and the Clyde made Glasgow, both being dependent on each other. The river rises in the Lanarkshire hills and flows the seventy miles to the sea through the city and what was once the heartland of the shipbuilding industry – GOVAN, PARTICK, WHITEINCH, SCOTSTOUN and CLYDEBANK and on to the Firth of Clyde. As the estuary of the Clyde was shallow and the deep-water ports were at DUMBARTON and IRVINE, so during the 18th and 19th centuries the Clyde was deepened and docks were built right up to the city centre, allowing merchant ships from all over the world to sail up to Glasgow. With this expansion of trade the city grew and by the early 1900s it was known as the *'Second City of the Empire'*, and thirty per cent of all the

Cranes on Govan Shipyard - Alex-McGregor

ships in the world were Clyde-built, a sign of superior workmanship and excellence, and an industry benchmark for quality. But not all the shipbuilders were situated on the Clyde; ALLEY & MACLELLAN'S SENTINEL WORKS were about half a mile from the water's edge in Jessie Street at POLMADIE.

THE TOBACCO LORDS

These wealthy merchants profited from trade with the tobacco plantations in **Virginia, Jamaica, Tobago** and **Antigua** between 1707 and the American War of Independence of 1775 to 1783. Glasgow was an excellent place to ply this trade as the sailing time to America was twenty days shorter from here than from London. Streets in the city reflect the influence of these countries and also the names of the Tobacco Lords such as DUNLOP STREET *(James Dunlop)*, INGRAM STREET *(Archibald Ingram)* and GLASSFORD STREET *(John Glassford)*. It is harder to find buildings associated with this trade but there is still the tobacco merchant's house at 42 MILLER STREET where ROBERT FINDLAY lived from 1780 to 1802. The foyer of **Glasgow's Gallery of Modern Art** used to be part of tobacco lord WILLIAM CUNNINGHAME'S mansion house and the BUCHANAN STREET entrance to the ARGYLE ARCADE was once part of a tobacco merchant's house.

GLASGOW
The Tobacco Merchant's House
John Craig
1775
LANDMARKS
42 Miller Street - Katherine Buchamnan

EDINBURGH

Edinburgh Castle sits proudly above the hustle and bustle of Scotland's capital city.

The rock on which it stands is only one of Edinburgh's several volcanic hills. Originally there were many lochs but the only one that remains today is DUDDINGSTON in **Holyroood Park.** The site of PRINCES STREET GARDENS used to be the *Nor' Loch*, which was formed in the 15th century as KING JAMES III wished this forested valley to be flooded to strengthen the castle's defences, and about this time Edinburgh was made the capital of Scotland.

The *Nor' Loch* may have started out as an asset to the residents of Edinburgh as they could boat across it and skate upon it in the winter. However, this loch had other sinister uses such as the *doukin' of witches*. The suspected witch would have her thumbs and toes tied together and be douked on a special stool, into the loch, not once but twice. This was really a no-win situation for if she sank and drowned she would be found innocent, but if she floated and survived she would be found guilty and burnt at the stake on CASTLEHILL. In the 16th century there were more burnings of witches here than anywhere else in Scotland. There is a plaque on the wall at WITCHES' WELL, near the entrance to the castle, in commemoration of over 300 women, accused of being witches, who were burnt at the stake.

This Fountain marks the spot where many witches were burned at the stake.

Katherine Buchanan

THE OLD TOWN

Originally, Edinburgh covered a small area around the castle and in 1385, when the city was set alight by Richard II of England, it consisted of 400 houses. As Edinburgh grew as a trading centre the High Street was the hub, and the pattern of long wynds running back at right angles from this street was formed by gardens that were later built over. By the middle of the 15th century, 35,000 people lived in this area. Buildings grew taller due to the restrictions of space and cellars were excavated below street level. Some of the buildings on the Royal Mile exceeded ten storeys high, making them the first skyscrapers! A good example of a high-rise tenement in the Royal Mile is the six-storied GLADSTONE'S LAND, built in the 17th century and now owned by the National Trust for Scotland. These high buildings were prone to falling down and above PAISLEY CLOSE, near

JOHN KNOX HOUSE, is the carving of the face of a young boy and an inscription which reads, *'Heave awa chaps, I'm no' dead yet.'* In 1861 a tenement collapsed killing 37 people, and just when the rescuers were about to give up they heard a voice crying out those words. They set to work once more and saved the trapped boy.

Paisley Close - Katherine Buchamnan

By the 1750s, Edinburgh was a booming trade centre and the Royal Exchange was built on top of several closes, including MARY KING'S CLOSE;

you can now book a guided tour of these underground closes. The building of the NEW TOWN attracted the wealthy merchants and professional classes and the OLD TOWN fell into a state of decay with people living in cramped, unsanitary conditions.

BANKING, BEER AND BISCUITS

The fortunes of Edinburgh were built on banking and the law and the industries of **beer**, **biscuits** and **publishing**. The nearby PORT OF LEITH gave access to world trading routes and this added to the city's prosperity.

Some of the Scots who influenced the banking system include JOHN NAPIER *(1550–1617)* of Merchiston, who introduced the decimal point as well as logarithms, which he described in his book in 1614. WILLIAM PATERSON came up with the idea to create the Bank of England and he published a paper with the proposal in 1691 and three years later the Bank of England was born. WILLIAM HOGG was an Edinburgh merchant who had a thriving business but sometimes had cash-flow problems when customers were slow to pay. He went along to the Royal Bank of Scotland, who proposed to let him be overdrawn for a short time as they appreciated that the money would be paid. This was the very first overdraft in the world and it happened in Edinburgh in 1728. During the 19th and 20th centuries there were around thirty-five breweries in Edinburgh. WILLIAM YOUNGER started off brewing in LEITH in 1749 and JOHN CRABBIE imported ginger from the Far East into the PORT OF LEITH in 1801 to make *Crabbie's Ginger Beer* and *Green Ginger Wine*. WILLIAM MCEWAN'S Fountain Brewery produced beer here from 1856 until the 1990s. The CALEDONIAN BREWERY, established by LORIMER and CLARK in 1869, continues brewing to this day with Deuchars IPA, popular with the author Ian Rankin and his character Inspector Rebus. The Edinburgh brewers, Innis and Gunn, discovered by accident the unique taste of oak-aged beer and one of the places you can buy this is the *Taste of Scotland* shop on North Bridge.

Robert McVitie and his father William opened a shop in Rose Street in 1830. Their baking proved to be so popular that it was not long before the family opened more shops. Charles Price joined the firm in 1875 and the large McVitie and Price factory opened in 1888. Alexander Grant de Forres, who worked for the company, devised and produced the original *Digestive Biscuit* in 1892. It was over thirty years before chocolate digestives appeared on the market, around the same time as the Jaffa Cake. Eventually this company amalgamated with Macfarlane Lang and is now United Biscuits.

The Highlands

The Scottish Highlands (or the *Hielands* as they are referred to in Scots; or *A' Ghàidhealtachd, 'the place of the Gaels'*, as they are called in Scottish Gaelic) have a rich history. Known for their beauty, these scenic lands have seen more than their fair share of drama and suffering. A big part of this was due to the history of the clans. Much depicted in films, the history of the Highland Clans and the battling chieftains is a violent one. Many people were killed and this period is certainly one of the darkest chapters in Scotland's past. So too were the battles with the English.

Up until the 19th century, many more people lived and worked in the Highlands than do today. But this all changed, for a number of reasons. The Highland way of life was outlawed after the Jacobite Rising of 1745.

iStock

iStock

Added to this were the HIGHLAND CLEARANCES, in which landowners cruelly evicted locals and took over their land. While some people emigrated, others ended working by the sea. Of those who migrated, many moved to Canada, the US and Australia. In fact, there are now more descendants from the Highlands living outside Scotland than there are living in the old country!

Another significant reason for the falling population of the Highlands was the migration of many to urban areas to seize the opportunities for employment offered by the INDUSTRIAL REVOLUTION. All this led to the Scottish Highlands becoming one of the least populated areas in Europe. In 2012, the number of people living in the Highlands and the Islands was less than a seventh of Scotland's population as a whole! However, recent projections suggest that if trends continue as they have been, the population in the Highlands should increase to 255,835 in 2035. That's a 15 per cent increase from 2010!

The Scottish Islands

Ancient, haunting, fascinating… the islands of Scotland hold a special draw for many people. Sparsely populated, these remote places contian countless clues to Scotland's past. For example, on the largest island in the ORKNEYS, Mainland, you can find SKARA BRAE, one of the most important prehistoric monuments in Europe which is, not surprisingly, referred to as the *'Scottish Pompeii'*.

Scotland has no fewer than 790 offshore islands in four main groups: **Shetland** (which is a group of around 100 islands) **Orkney** (around 70 islands) and the **Hebrides**, which are sub-divided into the **Inner Hebrides** and **Outer Hebrides**. Let's not forget ARRAN AND BUTE in the FIRTH OF CLYDE and the islands of ST. KILDA, 40 miles west of the Western Isles. Just some of Scotland's islands are:

Iona

Iona in the **Inner Hebrides** had a key role in the history of the monastic tradition in Scotland. The monastery was founded in AD 563 by ST. COLUMBA. It continues this tradition today through its well-known ecumenical retreat.

Foula

Foula in the **Shetlands** is known for only having adopted Scottish law in the 17th century. The ancient Norsk language *Norn* was spoken on the island up until the 19th century!

Jura

Jura is thought have gained its name from the Norse for *'deer island'*. History records that Jura was once home to around 300 deer; there are now around 7,000! Apart from one whisky distillery, Jura is known for being very sparsely populated and

iStock - Mike Lane

very quiet, not least because most of the island can only be visited on foot. GEORGE ORWELL spent some time living and working on Jura. It is where he completed *Nineteen Eighty-Four*. He described it as *'extremely ungetatable'*.

FAIR ISLE

The history of one of the remotest islands in the UK is closely connected with traditional knitwear. It's incredible that, despite a relative lack of resources, this skill has been practised continuously on the small island for generations. To knit using the traditional Fair Isle *'in the round'* method, knitters use double-pointed needles which are referred to as *'wires'*, with a padded knitting belt. While the origins of this skills have been lost in the mists of time, Fair Isle knitwear and its star motif trademark continues to be recognised the world over.